a glass act

a glass act

by ron morgan
photography by keith lewis

a glass act

For information, contact
Half Full Press
1814 Franklin Street, Suite 815
Oakland, CA 94612
(510) 839-5471

Editing/Design by Angie Hinh

10 09 08 07 06   1 2 3 4 5

ISBN 0-9719552-5-5

Printed and bound in China

To Rob Bond, the driving force
behind my book world

table of contents

▪ foreword

I am flattered to be writing this foreword for my friend Ron Morgan's latest book, *A Glass Act*. For those readers who already know his first two titles — *The Center of Attention* and *In the Company of Flowers* — you'll notice this one looks very different. Not only is it a different format, it's also the first time he's used containers consisting of the same material throughout.

Although the overall style of his designs in *A Glass Act* is pared down, sleek, and contemporary, the sheer diversity of these classy arrangements attest to Ron's incredible creativity. Nothing is hidden in these arrangements — what's going on below the water level is as impressive as what's happening above. Ron's designs in *A Glass Act* inspire without intimidating.

For as long as I've known Ron, I am still astounded by his ability to create extraordinary designs. Even when faced with impossible odds, he always manages to conjure up magical displays, sometimes almost out of nothing. I think that if you were to give him flowers well past their prime, he'd find some way to freeze dry them in a flash and turn them into fabulous looking displays without missing a beat. There are no auditions most days he's at work. His lectures are first-take performances, all the while accompanied by his entertaining and informative commentary.

In *A Glass Act*, his elegant, inventive displays speak for themselves. Ron's chosen to impose his own editing process by using only undecorated glass containers. In some arrangements, he's adopted a "just picked and displayed in a simple container" look that many modern brides find appealing. Elegant simplicity — perfect for our times.

Ron is renowned for his generosity and is very supportive of his friends. He and I have just collaborated on a book together — *A Celebration of Clematis*. My first book, I was swept along with his enthusiasm and creative energy. To my amazement, the project was finished on schedule with a mere four months of production. Then scarcely without a pause to draw breath, Ron started on this new book project.

A Glass Act demonstrates his flexibility and the breadth of his abilities. Celebrating flower forms, mixed textures, and colors, the sheer inventiveness of many of these designs show that his creativity knows no bounds. It's the sign of a real artist at work. I think you'll agree with me when I assert that, with *A Glass Act*, he has done it again. It's a real class act. Well done, Ron!

Kaye Heafey

I've always loved flowers. Ever since I can remember, I've been drawn to their captivating beauty, color, and fragrance. Fortunately, my environment nurtured this innate love of mine, setting the stage for my lifelong relationship with these exquisite fruits of nature.

My childhood was filled with fabulous gardeners. My grandparents, aunts, great-aunts, and father were all avid lovers of flora and fauna who lovingly tended their gardens. I would often visit my father's aunt in the Midwest and admire her mesmerizing natural garden, spending hours on end wandering through endless rows of extraordinary flowers. Back at home in Stockton, CA, I would help my father create life and beauty within his own garden. Together, my father and I would plant seedlings, nourish them, watch them grow, and eventually harvest them.

We had a wonderful neighbor when I was a kid growing up who always entered the annual San Joaquin County Fair with prize blooms that she had mothered to perfection. Being naturally drawn to the flower arranging scene, I went out with her a couple of times — the first being when I was barely ten years old — and entered my own amateur arrangements in the fair. To my surprise and delight, I ended up winning several blue ribbons! I thought to myself, "You know, this is kind of fun!" So, throughout the years that followed, I just kept it up. I had always wanted to go to art school, and, through this delightful county fair experience, I discovered that flowers were my way to do sculpture, just with plant material.

My career as a lecturer started as a fluke. The garden club had a huge convention in Oakland years and years ago; one of my girl friends from the garden club took me as her guest to this event. The woman hosting the convention was from Cleveland — she was the high mucky-muck of flowers in those days. She gave this whole extended talk on flower arranging. Back then, flower arranging was very rigid; it had to be this wide and go in this space and be this tall, etcetera, etcetera, etcetera. While I was not especially impressed with the rigidity she endorsed, I nevertheless decided to make the most of things and took notes.

That night, my girl friend called me and said, "Could you do a talk tomorrow?" My immediate response was, "No, that's stupid, there's no way I can do a talk tomorrow." She replied, "Well, somebody has to, because the woman who was supposed to do the talk tomorrow fell in the bathtub and broke her arm in the hotel tonight." "Well, shoot," I thought, "somebody needs to step up to the plate here!" So I said, "Yeah, I'll do it!" I spent all night in my parents' basement making things three times as tall as the container but skinny, so that the proportion was right, and I went to my girl friend the next day and said, "Look, I don't mean to offend you, but things can be done differently and look right proportion-wise and color-wise." After reviewing my work, she was just so fascinated that she right then and there exclaimed, "I'm taking you with me!" So I went back to Cleveland, Cincinnati, Toledo, etc. and started doing garden club talks all back East. From there everything just mushroomed — now it's once a week somewhere!

For me, arranging is all about doing justice to the flowers

themselves: I love things that are very classic and pretty. I don't like all this "flowers in bondage" and some of this way-out bizarre stuff. I like flowers that are just pretty. To complement the flowers' natural elegance, I've always incorporated fruits, vegetables, and seedpods into my arrangements. Basically, all produce is either a seedpod or a bud from a flower — it's all part of the same plant chain. I love the combination! I think nothing is prettier than a single flower nestled in its own seedpod and its own foliage. God made very few mistakes — the leaves, the seedpods, and the flowers just look good together! I like things that are kind of gutsy, and sometimes the big produce and seedpods give my arrangements that kind of gutsy feeling; I don't like flowers that are too ethereal and fluffy. I like things that make a statement. Over the years I've found that the challenge with arranging is constantly coming up with something new, fresh, and fun. Above all, I try to just keep it light and enjoy it every day — for heaven's sake, don't take it too seriously! For me, it's still play — after forty-five years I still love what I do!

A Glass Act is an attempt to make the joy of floral arranging accessible to everyone. A lot of young kids nowadays don't have time to do flowers; everybody wants flowers in their homes, but a lot of the young working girls don't have time to sit and fiddle with flowers all day long. Glass containers are very popular now — everybody's loving glass! The hardest part of using glass is the mechanics of it, because you see everything — nothing's hidden, everything's exposed. But I love the luminous quality, I love being able to see through it, how it magnifies things, the little bubbles attached to the flowers — it's almost like making little sculptures in cubes encased in Lucite! The wonderful truth is that there's some very fun, simple things you can do with glass that anybody can just pick up, do, and say "Oh gosh, isn't that fun!"

My advice to all aspiring and seasoned arrangers: have fun, don't take it seriously, don't try to follow rules too closely — I think they shouldn't be called rules anyhow, because when you start following rules for flower arranging, it almost puts you off; they should be called something more gentle like "guidelines," as opposed to something frightening like "rules" — but just have fun, do what suits you in your house. You have to live with it; nobody else does.

I love what I do because flowers make people smile; every time I do a wedding or a party everybody says "Oh, it's so pretty!" It just makes people happy, which to me makes all the difference.

Ron Morgan

The word "glass" brings to mind mirrors, glasses, prisms, windows — all media through which we can experience reality in a slightly different way than that allotted through the lens of ordinary experience. Combined with color, glass holds a captivating power; through glass, colors merge into one another, seeming somehow more vibrant, more enhanced, more alive than they appear to be without the aid of the shimmering screen. By establishing a barrier of glass between us and the fantastic, mysterious world of nature, we can, ironically, feel closer to that beauty which surrounds us in our everyday lives.

green

She runs through the meadow at dusk, the wet grass brushing playfully at her bare ankles. Crickets chirp in the gathering shadows as the light begins to fade and nature prepares to wrap its young in an inky blanket. Yet through the shadows the soft green tint of the old oak can still be perceived, waving its leaves faintly in the gentle breeze, bidding her goodnight, sleep tight for tomorrow is a new day filled with laughter and love and life.

Green is, by all accounts, representative of the miracle of life itself. If there were a tangible goddess of nature, she would undoubtedly don a gown of shimmering green. Harmony in nature, growth, and natural freshness immediately come to mind when contemplating this color. On the flip side, green has traditionally been associated with immaturity and childish jealousies. The association is logical enough, as envy exemplifies dissatisfaction with what is and a desire to grow into what could be.

3

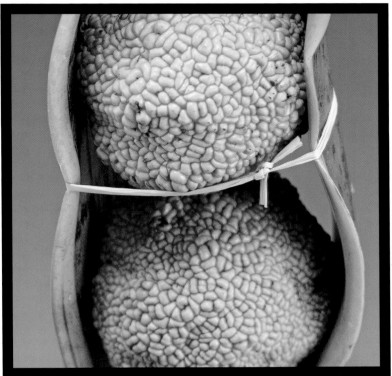

 pink

The rose garden is her favorite place. Every so often, when her ailing mother is sleeping and her young son is away at school, she comes and sits here on the old wooden bench, admiring the tranquil beauty of the blushing roses and inhaling their musky scent. Her hands, weathered by time but nonetheless delicate, rest in the lap of her pink flower-print summer dress. So much time has passed since she first discovered this garden — why, she had been just a girl! But is it noon already? She stands, her unassuming cotton dress falling gracefully around her thighs. She must attend to the luncheon! . . . Perhaps she'll bring some roses.

Pink is for presentation. A Real Lady would never be caught wearing red at a high-class gathering, but pink, on the other hand, is perfectly acceptable. Pink represents a softness, a delicacy, a sense of refinement; rather than inciting disorder, pink neutralizes it. Traditionally, pink is associated with tenderness, caring, and acceptance. Like a white gossamer curtain overlaying a discarded red garment, pink soothes the savage beast typically evoked by its sister shade.

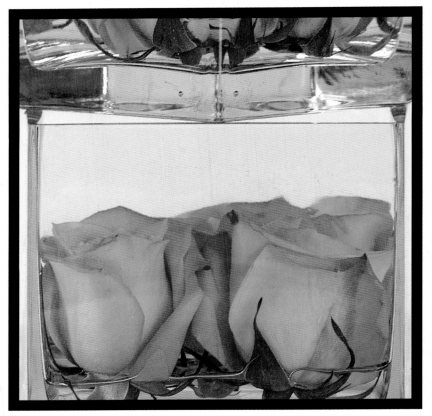

brown

Bare-footed and brazen she stepped out onto the precipice, with only her worn woolen blanket shielding her against the winter wind. And what if she were to jump? What then? The unruly sea roared below her, tumultuous yet undeniably inviting. Mother was sick; father was a drunkard; would she really be missed? Her long mousy brown hair whipped feverishly around her wan features as she took a step forward, towards the jutting edge. And yet . . . She wrapped the coarse rust-colored blanket more tightly around her and raked the barren landscape with her hollow gray eyes. The sea beckons, she thought, but so does the ramshackle rocking chair by the fire.

Brown is romantic in its own way. Connoting a definite bareness and lack-of-ness, the color exudes a kind of solid, devil-may-care, down-to-earth quality that holds a distinct kind of timeless charm. More so than purple, brown connotes a steady strength; a "brown" person could always be relied upon to come through, to carry on in the most trying of times. It is a color that brings us back to our roots, that — perhaps even more so than green — truly unifies us with nature, living and non-living elements alike. With this in mind, one can't help but recognize that brown is undeniably a beautiful color.

Slowly she wraps her soft, silky fingers around the base of the crystal glass half full with Merlot. 9:15, the cherry wood clock says; 9:15, and he has not arrived. Out with another woman, perhaps? Or simply held up by his wife? She wraps her scarlet shawl more tightly around her bare white shoulders and sips the rich, dark wine, pursing her moist crimson lips slightly to better savor the flavor. Not to worry; she knew he would come. And if he didn't . . . well, there was always the 11:30 appointment.

Red is the spokesman for the spiciness in life. Red evokes heat in all its forms: romance, violence, rawness, and sultriness. Red is what men see when they are angry and what women feel when they are lustful. It is the flush rising in a deflowered maiden's formerly pallid cheeks; it is the spark glinting in the revolutionary's eye as he rallies his troops. Red is, essentially, fire; while its literal form indisputably contains an awesome power, it appears to be most potent in its figurative form — that is, the form residing within the human breast.

□ white

One. Two. Three. The church bell tolls, calling the penitent to arms. Four. Five. There is to be a wedding today — a small affair, just the bride, the groom, and close family and friends. Six. Seven. She wanted lilies, she said; white lilies, and perhaps some roses. Clematis would be nice, too. Eight. Oh, but the dress — the dress was exquisite: luminous pearls draped elegantly down its sides, like precious tears of happiness frozen in time. Nine. Today: today, she is a bride. Ten.

White is, of course, traditionally associated with purity, cleanliness, and innocence. A white canvas has not yet been painted on; a white napkin has not yet been stained. As we live in an inherently unclean, impure mortal world (for all its magnificence), it is no surprise that white is often associated with reverence to some higher, holier power, or religious devotion. White therefore is undoubtedly the most powerful color, precisely because it evokes a humbleness that has frequently been wielded as a weapon in a variety of social circles throughout history.

■ burgundy

Through-under-up-out comes the needle . . . Did you know my Jane is going to Princeton? She is so smart, I always said so, she got into Harvard, did you know that? But she decided to go to Princeton instead . . . through-under-up-out-St-it-ch . . . Oh yes, I remember Jane, short black hair, was it? Always crazy about the boys, I recall . . . through-under-up-out-St-it-ch . . . Oh I nearly forgot to tell you — my Matthew — remember him? He was at Bertha's Christmas Party, such a handsome boy — Matthew is engaged to that Swanson girl who lives down the street! . . . through-under-up-out-St-it-ch . . . The Swanson girl? But she's so . . . So duck-like, with those feet of hers! . . . Really, with Matthew? . . . I know, it's a shame, it is . . . through-under-up-out-St-it-ch . . . But they say that love is blind, and this is proof if there ever was any . . . I dare say I would very much like to have some tea; would anyone care to put the kettle on? . . . through-under-up-out-St-it-ch . . .

Burgundy is a comfortable color. It is reminiscent of overstuffed, frilly couches and chamomile tea. Though not traditionally associated with anything in particular, burgundy nevertheless stands on its own symbolically. Perhaps its qualities bear the strongest resemblance to purple — rather than a young and powerful queen, an aged, frumpy, doddering, yet nonetheless lovable queen comes to mind. Burgundy lends itself well to caricature; of all the colors, it is certainly the most difficult to take seriously.

■ orange

The bright lights of the carnival wink impishly in the darkness. They run hand in hand, giggling, streamers in their hair and colorful beads bouncing against their chests. Tonight is for them, only them — to be free, to be alive, to feel the electricity surging unchecked through their veins . . . Oh youth! She wraps her thin arms around his neck as he spins her around, faster faster faster until the bright lights swirl together into one blurry mass of color, and she steps down, laughing, her face flushed a pale pink that matches her playful dress. Run away with me, he said. Run away with me to the carnival where we'll dance every day and smell roses every night and you can be my true love now and forever. Yes, she says, the soft breeze blowing kisses through her hair. Yes.

Orange is pure energy. A mixture between red and yellow, it shares qualities with both colors: like red, it is unbridled and fierce; like yellow, is has a warm, youthful quality about it. While yellow brings to mind the buoyancy of a child, orange connotes the still-innocent ephemeral nature of a developing adolescent. Only orange can exemplify the electric excitement of awakening to the sensory world in all its possibilities.

purple

The streets of San Francisco hum with activity as she walks down Market Street, her heels clicking methodically against the concrete pavement. Another day at the office; another day immersed in the trials and tribulations of the corporate world. Her stiff silk suit constrains her posture as she walks, making her appear to be more of a presence than a person. She observes the bustle around her through violet-tinted Gucci shades. Who are these people that she sees every day, going about their idle business? What goes through their minds? Her mauve-colored lip curls slightly in a wry smile as she contemplates the world around her. A fellow who could fully comprehend the mind of another human being would be a powerful fellow indeed.

Purple is perhaps the most complex color, symbolically speaking: while it traditionally represents wealth and power, its very nature — being a mixture between icy blue and sultry red — warrants it an emblem of instability and veiled unrest. It simultaneously connotes royalty and spirituality, self-sufficiency and neediness; a queen befriending a pauper, a lonely princess spurning her numerous eager suitors, a proud Siamese cat sauntering over in an unassuming manner for a much-desired loving pat on the head. Purple evokes veiled — not suppressed, but merely controlled, manipulated, and directed — passions. It thus comes as no surprise that purple is also traditionally associated with artistic and creative genius.

yellow

Soft sunlight spills through the window onto the tawny head of a seven-year-old girl. Her hair is pulled back in a sloppy ponytail, displaying a careless innocence that she would soon grow out of. Splayed on the beige carpet in a disorderly fashion are a dozen or so little yellow flowers. Her modest pink lips pursed in concentration, the girl picks up one of the blossoms, dabs some Elmer's on its back, and plops it down on a sheaf of light green construction paper. The girl grins, pleased with her handiwork. Scrawled lovingly in the center of the paper are the carefully executed words "Happy Mother's Day!"

Like bright rays on a sunny day, yellow typically evokes warmth, joy, and unadulterated happiness. When one thinks of yellow, one can't help but think of a kind of lightness of being, a kind of carefree youthfulness that comes and goes when it pleases but cannot be reined in. A child, hitherto untarnished by any shadowy rays, exemplifies yellow. Interestingly enough, yellow is also representative of cowardice and deceit — qualities that, granted, do require a certain amount of psychological removal from the confines of social expectations.

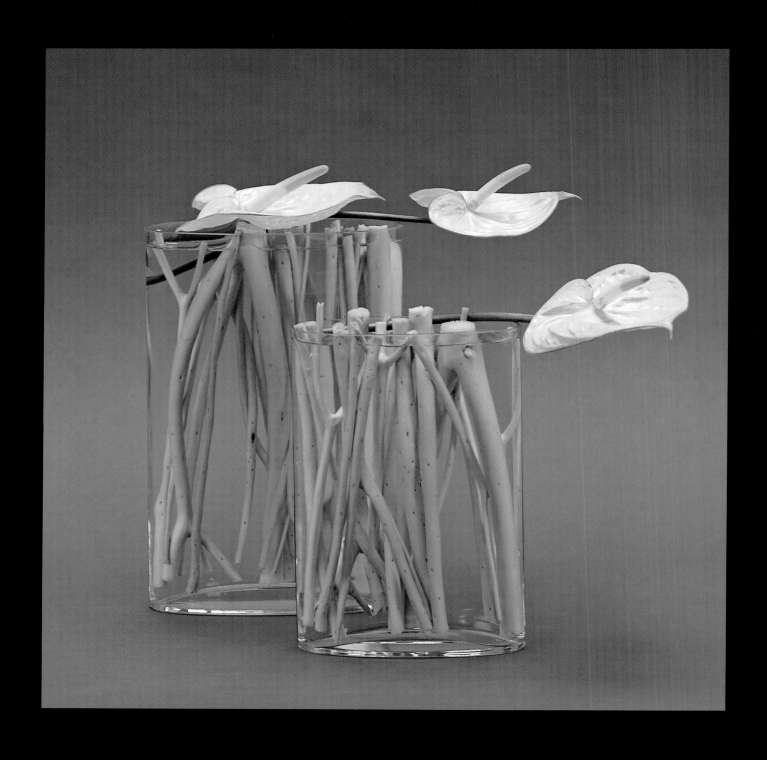

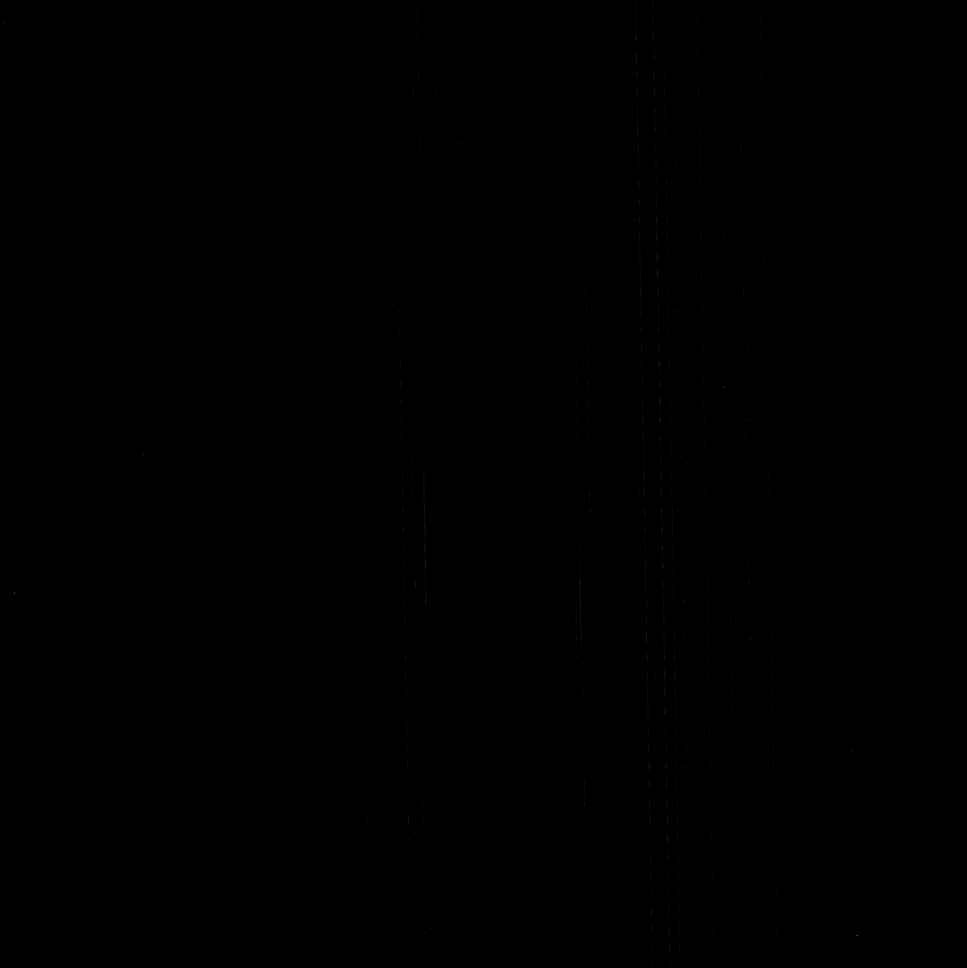

At the end of the road, the night awaits: silent, watchful, brooding — and beautiful. Beautiful, for it gives the mind's eye the opportunity to blossom into its full richness, unhindered by the constraints of illumination. Night is the domain of imagination, conception, creation. We dream during the twilight hours, only to realize those dreams with the coming of day in a rainbow of color and glass.

captions

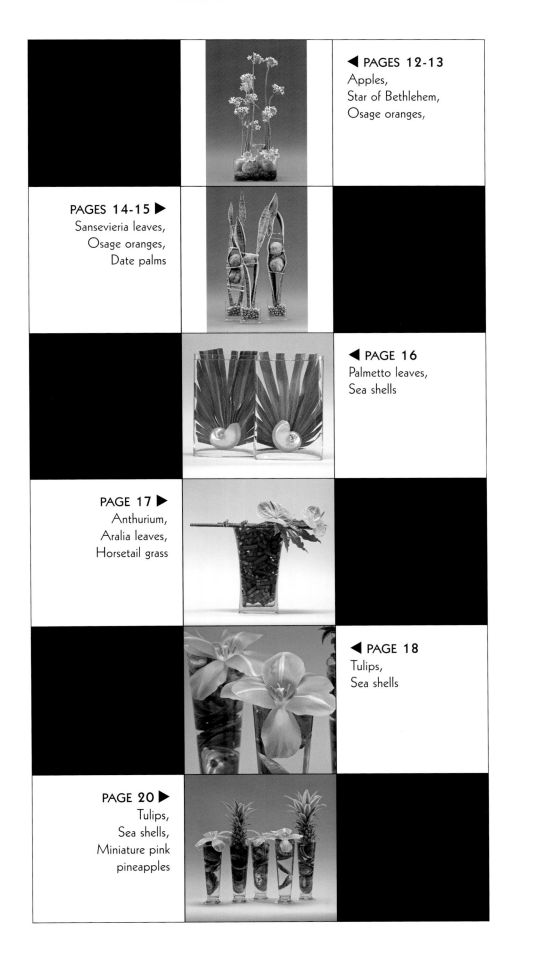

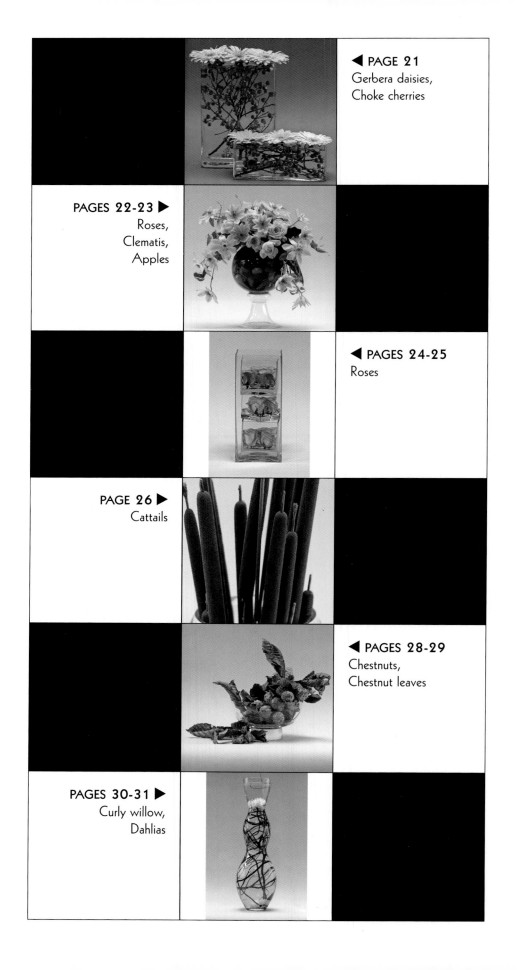

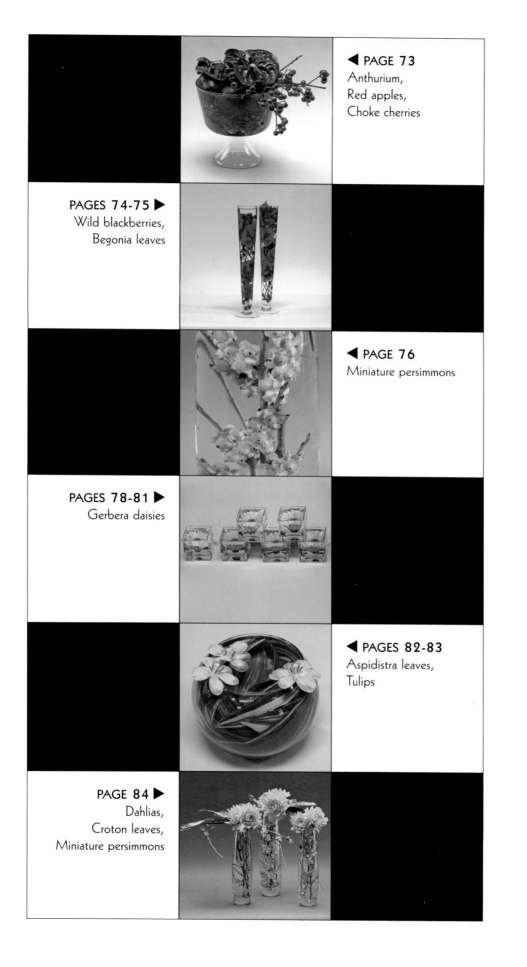

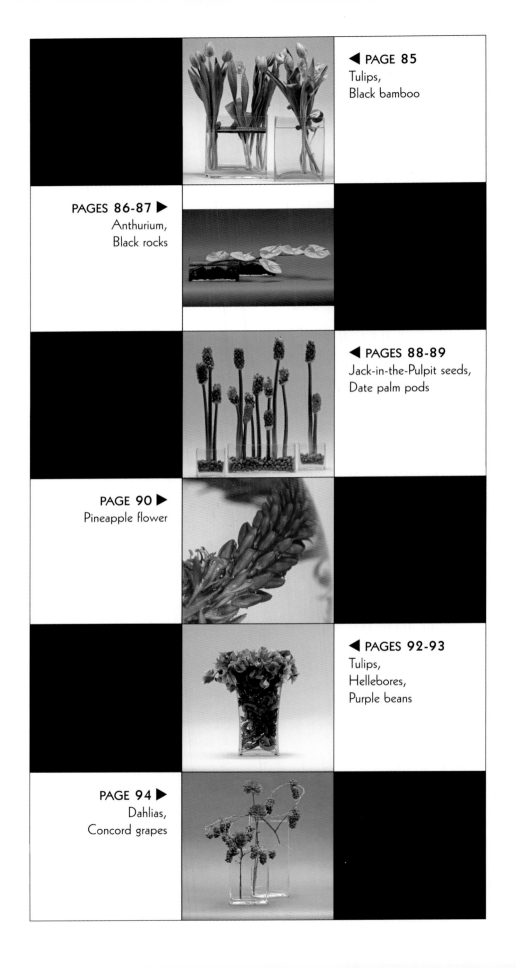

◀ PAGES 116-117
Cymbidium orchids,
Bittersweet,
Osage oranges

ron's flower care tips

- To ensure longer flower life, cut most flowers when the color begins to show in the bud.
- Cut flowers in the morning, when the maximum amount of moisture is in the stem.
- Always cut flowers with a sharp knife. Roses should be cut under water. To ensure that the maximum amount of water is available to the flowers, cut the stems at a diagonal (poppies being an exception). Use warm water — at least room temperature.
- Most hard or wood stems should either be cut with shears or mashed with a hammer before placing them into the water.
- For a longer lifespan, remove most of the foliage from flowers.
- Do not leave flowers standing in bright, direct sunlight as they will wilt faster.
- To ensure crispness, submerge large flowers like hydrangeas and dahlias in water for a few minutes.
- Use wooden (as opposed to metal) skewers to hold elements of a table setting together. The wood expands and therefore has better holding power.
- Use oil of cloves or oil of cinnamon on the tip of a wooden pick before inserting into fruits and vegetables. This will make them last longer.
- Do not pack flowers too tightly into containers. Oxygen needs to get to the water's surface so that the flowers can breathe properly.
- Never have foliage below the water line of the container. Foliage tends to rot when in direct contact with water and this will shorten the lives of the remaining flowers.
- Most flowers do not like metal containers, as oxides are released from the containers into the water.
- Use a fixative aerosol (a spray for charcoal or pastel paintings) on cut fruit to prevent flies and insects.
- A shot of Sprite, or similar sugary soda, does wonders in bringing tired flowers back to life.
- Although it is preferable to change water daily for arrangements, it is not always practical. When it is not possible, use one teaspoon of bleach per gallon of flower water to kill the resulting bacteria. As the stems take oxygen from the water, a bacteria-ridden scum is produced. This bacteria is the single most harmful thing for all flowers. The easiest way to add water to existing floral arrangements is with a turkey baster.

131